D0417011

The Life and World of

CLEOPATRA

Struan Reid

Heinemann
LIBRARY

www.heinemann.co.uk/library
Visit our website to find out more information about Heinemann Library books.

To order:
☎ Phone 44 (0) 1865 888066
▤ Send a fax to 44 (0) 1865 314091
🖥 Visit the Heinemann Library Bookshop at www.heinemann.co.uk/library to browse our catalogue and order online.

First published in Great Britain by Heinemann Library,
Halley Court, Jordan Hill, Oxford OX2 8EJ
a division of Reed Educational and Professional Publishing Ltd.
Heinemann is a registered trademark of Reed Educational & Professional Publishing Ltd.

OXFORD MELBOURNE AUCKLAND
JOHANNESBURG BLANTYRE GABORONE
IBADAN PORTSMOUTH (NH) USA CHICAGO

Designed by Celia Floyd
Illustrated by Jeff Edwards and Joanna Brooker
Originated by Ambassador Litho Ltd
Printed in Hong Kong by Wing King Tong.

ISBN 0 431 14774 4
06 05 04 03 02
10 9 8 7 6 5 4 3 2 1

British Library Cataloguing in Publication Data

Reid, Struan
  The life and world of Cleopatra
  1. Cleopatra, Queen of Egypt, d. 30 B.C.
  2. Queens – Egypt – Biography – Juvenile literature
  3. Egypt – History – 332-30 B.C. – Juvenile literature
  I. Title   II. Cleopatra
  932'.021'092

Acknowledgements

The Publishers would like to thank the following for permission to reproduce photographs: AKG: pp10, 20, 28; Ancient Art and Architecture: p18; Ancient Egypt Picture Library: p13; The Art Archive: pp7, 12; Associated Press: p29; Bildarchive: p22; British Museum: pp6, 11, 15, 26; Trevor Clifford: p19; Corbis: p16; Corbis/Archivo Iconografico, S.A.: p27; Corbis/Roger Wood: pp8, 17; Louvre/Agence Photographique de la Reunion des Musees Nationaux: pp9, 25; Metropolitan Museum of Art: p24; National Trust: p21; Scala: p14; University of Glasgow Hunterian Museum: p4; The Worshipful Company of Goldsmiths: p23.

Cover photograph reproduced with permission of AKG.

Our thanks to Rebecca Vickers for her help in the preparation of this book.

Every effort has been made to contact copyright holders of any material reproduced in this book. Any omissions will be rectified in subsequent printings if notice is given to the Publisher.

Contents

Any words appearing in the text in bold, **like this**,
are explained in the glossary.

Who was Cleopatra?

The name of Cleopatra is one of the most famous in history. Cleopatra (about 70–30 BC) was the last queen of Egypt. She was born into the royal family that had ruled Egypt for nearly 300 years.

Egypt and Rome

When Cleopatra was born Egypt was a very rich country, but it was very badly ruled. The real power in the area was Rome, the centre of the **Roman Empire**. Cleopatra fought to preserve her royal family and the independence of Egypt. From a very early age she showed that she was cunning and clever, both important in a difficult and dangerous world. At the height of her power, Cleopatra made even mighty Rome tremble. She lived an action-packed life, and died when she was only about 39 years old.

How do we know?

We know much about Cleopatra and her times because she lived in one of the most exciting and important periods in world history. **Historians** have left us many written records. Much of the information, though, was written by her enemies in Rome. These writers describe her as an evil, **scheming** woman. Anything written by Cleopatra's supporters was probably destroyed after she died. Some of the most important information about Cleopatra was written by a Greek historian called Plutarch, who lived 100 years after Cleopatra. He, too, had to rely on the accounts written by her enemies.

◀ Cleopatra has always been described as beautiful, although coins showing her portrait may tell a different story. More important than her looks, though, was her great intelligence.

What did Cleopatra look like?

Most of the statues of Cleopatra were pulled down after her death, so we do not really know what she looked like. However, coins with her portrait on them have survived. These can give us some idea of her appearance. **Archaeologists** keep discovering objects which show Cleopatra. From these we can learn more about what she looked like.

▶ Egypt was a rich and powerful nation for thousands of years before Cleopatra was born. When she was queen, however, she had to fight hard to keep her nation **independent**.

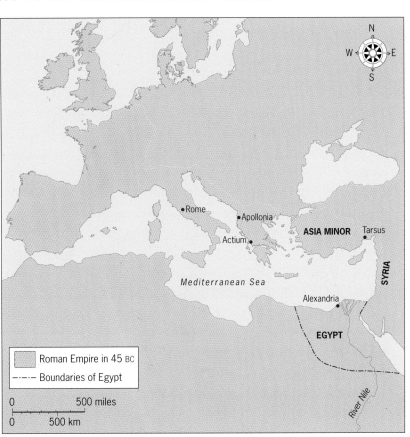

Roman Empire in 45 BC
-·-·- Boundaries of Egypt

0   500 miles
0   500 km

Key dates

305 BC	Ptolemy I founds (starts) the **Ptolemaic** royal **dynasty**, the family of Cleopatra
About 70 BC	Cleopatra is born
51 BC	Cleopatra becomes Queen of Egypt
30 BC	Death of Cleopatra
30 BC	Egypt becomes part of the Roman Empire

Watch the dates
BC after a year date means before the birth of Jesus Christ. The years are counted backwards to zero, the date of Christ's birth.

Princess Cleopatra

Cleopatra was born in the Egyptian capital city of Alexandria in about 70 BC. She was the daughter of King Ptolemy XII of Egypt. When she was born, Egypt was still a rich, **independent** country. Across the Mediterranean Sea in Italy, though, Rome was becoming more and more powerful. Many **nations** were conquered, and the **Roman Empire** was spreading.

Cleopatra's family

King Ptolemy XII had several different wives. He had four daughters and two sons. We do not know exactly who Cleopatra's mother was. She may have been King Ptolemy's own sister, Cleopatra Tryphaina. It was the custom in Egypt for the king to marry his sister. Cleopatra had two older sisters, one also called Cleopatra and the other called Berenice. She had one younger sister called Arsinoe. Her two younger brothers later ruled as Ptolemy XIII and Ptolemy XIV.

Cleopatra's father was not a good king. All the different princes and princesses fought for power and influence. Egypt was growing poorer and poorer because it was ruled so badly. The people became angry, too, because they had to pay higher and higher taxes.

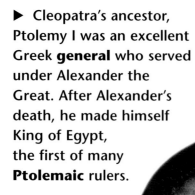

▶ Cleopatra's ancestor, Ptolemy I was an excellent Greek **general** who served under Alexander the Great. After Alexander's death, he made himself King of Egypt, the first of many **Ptolemaic** rulers.

Playing a dangerous game

Cleopatra soon learned how to play the dangerous games that were needed in order to survive in such difficult circumstances. Even the life of a royal princess was not safe. If Cleopatra found herself on the wrong side she might easily have been sent away from Egypt or, even worse, murdered.

▶ Alexander the Great was only a young man when he set out to increase Greek power. He conquered many nations, including Egypt, before he died aged 33.

Ancient Egypt

In 332 BC the Greek king and military leader Alexander the Great conquered Egypt. He created a new capital city on the shores of the Mediterranean Sea, which he named Alexandria after himself. After Alexander's death in 323 BC, Egypt was ruled by one of his **generals**, called Ptolemy. Ptolemy declared himself King Ptolemy I of Egypt in 305 BC. His family ruled Egypt for nearly 300 years until the death of Cleopatra, the last queen of Egypt.

Growing up in Alexandria

When Cleopatra was born, Alexandria, the capital city of Egypt, was one of the most important and beautiful cities in the world. It was a great centre of learning. Scientists, poets and **philosophers** travelled long distances to study at the museum, one of the world's first **universities**.

▼ When Cleopatra was queen, Alexandria was the capital city of Egypt, an important centre of learning and **trade**. Today it is a busy city.

Growing up

Cleopatra was brought up in a beautiful palace with hundreds of rooms and halls. They had marble walls, and were decorated with paintings and sculptures. Cleopatra, her sisters and brothers were looked after by an army of servants. Cleopatra did not go to school, but was given lessons by a private **tutor**. She was very clever and quickly learned many subjects, such as mathematics and poetry. She also learned to speak many languages. She was the only **Ptolemaic** ruler who spoke Egyptian. Most of her family could only speak Greek.

Ptolemy XII

Cleopatra's father, Ptolemy XII, had become king of Egypt in 80 BC, ten years before she was born. By 58 BC the Egyptian people were fed up with him and drove him out of the country. He fled to Rome, leaving his children behind in Alexandria. At this time Cleopatra was about twelve years old.

▶ Ptolemy XII, Cleopatra's father, was a very unpopular king with the Egyptian people. It was only Roman support that helped him to stay in power.

Family fighting

When Ptolemy XII fled to Rome in 58 BC, he was replaced as ruler by his second daughter, Berenice. His first daughter had died. Berenice did everything she could to stop her father coming back to Egypt. In 55 BC, three years later, Roman armies helped Ptolemy XII to return to power. The Romans supported him because they wanted to have some control over Egypt, which was a very rich and important **nation**. He immediately had Berenice and her supporters put to death.

Cleopatra the queen

Ptolemy XII was king of Egypt for another four years. He was still hated by the Egyptian people and he was only kept in power by the Roman army. In the spring of 51 BC he finally died. In his **will** he had named Cleopatra and his elder son as his **successors**. By rights, only his son should have succeeded, but Cleopatra was too strong and clever to be ignored. According to Egyptian custom, Cleopatra married the elder of her two brothers, who took the name Ptolemy XIII. They ruled Egypt together.

Queen Cleopatra

Cleopatra was now about nineteen, and Ptolemy XIII was only about nine or ten years old. The two hated each other. They quickly worked to gather their own supporters.

Because Cleopatra was ten years older than her brother, she felt that she should be able to rule Egypt on her own. Although he was too young to rule, Ptolemy XIII had many advisers and supporters who did not want Cleopatra to have her way.

◄ Although Cleopatra was a queen, the Egyptian people worshipped her as a goddess. Here, she is shown as the Egyptian goddess, Isis.

Not only was Cleopatra older and much more experienced than her brother, she was also extremely ambitious. She was determined to make Egypt a great **nation** again. However, whenever they could, young Ptolemy XIII's advisers tried to attack her. As she became more powerful, they became more frightened. They were determined to remove her from power. This struggle went on for three years. Finally, in 48 BC, when Cleopatra was about 22, Ptolemy XIII and his supporters managed to drive her out of Egypt.

▶ This gold ring has the cartouche (seal) of a **Ptolemaic** king.

The queen's enemies

Three enemies in particular drove Cleopatra out. The most powerful man in the royal palace was a Greek called Potheinos. He was the chief adviser to young Ptolemy XIII. The second most important person was an Egyptian called Achillas, who was captain of the royal guards. The third supporter of Ptolemy XIII was another Greek called Theodotos, who was the young king's **tutor**.

A dramatic entrance

When Cleopatra was forced out of Egypt by her enemies she fled eastward to Syria. There she gathered together an army of her own supporters. She planned to fight her way back to Egypt and regain power.

As Cleopatra was preparing to march back to Egypt with her army, events took a sudden and unexpected turn. Julius Caesar, one of the most powerful people in Rome, arrived in Alexandria. Fighting had broken out in the **Roman Empire**, and Julius Caesar had sailed to Egypt to fight his enemy, Gnaeus Pompeius Magnus, known as Pompey. When Caesar reached Egypt, he discovered that Pompey had been murdered by his own soldiers.

More fighting

The fighting in the Roman Empire had ended but another war now broke out in Egypt between the supporters of Cleopatra and the supporters of Ptolemy XIII on the other. As the leader of the greatest power in the area, Caesar tried to get the two sides to make peace. Ptolemy XIII agreed to meet Caesar in Alexandria, but he refused to allow his sister to return to Egypt. He threatened to have her killed if she dared to enter the country. Cleopatra was not to be defeated. She hatched a plan to outwit her brother.

▶ This Roman pavement mosaic from about 150 AD shows Roman soldiers beside the River Nile, in Egypt.

A secret meeting

Cleopatra sailed in secret from Syria across the Mediterranean Sea towards Egypt. During the night, before the ship reached the coast, Cleopatra climbed into another, smaller boat and sailed quietly into Alexandria. A servant called Apollodorus rolled her up in a blanket. He carried her past Ptolemy XIII's guards and straight into the royal palace where Caesar was staying. The blanket was placed on the floor in front of Caesar. As Apollodorus unrolled it Cleopatra tumbled out at the great leader's feet.

▼ These models of Egyptian soldiers were found in a tomb.

The greatest power

The fighting in the Roman Empire between Julius Caesar and Pompey altered the whole course of history. Julius Caesar introduced changes to how Rome was ruled. Because of these changes, for the next 400 years the Roman Empire was one of the greatest powers the world had ever seen. Egypt would soon be caught up in these great events.

Caesar meets his match

Julius Caesar must have been amazed when he saw Cleopatra unrolled before him. At this time he was aged 52 and Cleopatra was about 22 years old. The difference in their ages did not matter. They were powerful, but they were also fascinated by the power and ambition they saw in each other.

What impressed Caesar so much was Cleopatra's great intelligence and learning. Women at this time were usually not respected by men, but Cleopatra expected to be treated as an equal, even by the most powerful man in the Western world. From their first meeting, Cleopatra and Julius Caesar began one of the greatest love stories in history.

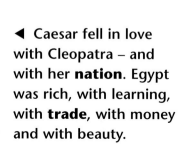

◄ Caesar fell in love with Cleopatra – and with her **nation**. Egypt was rich, with learning, with **trade**, with money and with beauty.

The death of Ptolemy

Caesar still hoped to bring peace to Egypt. But Ptolemy's soldiers attacked the palace where Cleopatra lived with Caesar. After six months of attacks against his soldiers, Caesar decided that he would put up with no more. His army defeated Ptolemy XIII's army near the banks of the River Nile. The young king tried to escape and jumped into a small boat. There were so many other soldiers on board that it capsized. Ptolemy XIII was thrown into the river and quickly drowned, weighed down by his suit of gold armour. He was about fifteen years old.

Cleopatra was now the only ruler of Egypt. She was crowned queen again. This time she took her youngest brother, now named Ptolemy XIV, as her new **co-ruler**. Because he was only twelve years old, Cleopatra was definitely the one in charge – just as she had always planned to be.

▲ Cleopatra may have been young, but she was clever and brave. This ancient silver coin from Alexandria shows the queen aged about 24.

Blessed by the gods

The Egyptians believed that anyone who was drowned in the River Nile, and whose body was lost in its waters, was especially blessed by the gods. It was very important for Cleopatra and Caesar to prove to the Egyptian people that Ptolemy XIII had not received this blessing. They had to make sure that Ptolemy's body was found and taken out of the river.

Plans to rule the Western world

After the fighting between Cleopatra and Ptolemy XIII was over, many Romans believed that Egypt should be made part of the **Roman Empire**, but Julius Caesar agreed to allow Egypt to remain as an **independent nation**. It soon became obvious to everyone that Cleopatra only managed to stay in power because she had the support of the Roman army.

Cruising the Nile

When Caesar first arrived in Alexandria he had planned to stay for just a short time, but he was dazzled by Egypt's ancient history and great wealth. Early in 47 BC, Cleopatra took Caesar on a cruise up the River Nile, travelling with a great number of ships and soldiers. They travelled in a beautiful royal barge, and watched the magnificent temples and palaces built along the shores of the River Nile glide past them.

▲ Cleopatra knew how to travel in style. As her people watched her barge float by on the River Nile, they would have worshipped her even more. This nineteenth-century French painting shows how the artist imagined it looked.

◄ The Egyptians worshipped many different gods. They believed that the gods lived in magnificent temples, such as this one they had built in Karnak.

Even though Cleopatra had won the battle against her enemies, there were still many Egyptians who hated her. She hoped that by sailing up the River Nile with so many ships and soldiers she would make it very clear to everyone that she was in charge. They would realize that she would not tolerate any more fighting.

Caesar's new plans

The cruise on the River Nile was also a kind of public celebration for Caesar. New plans were beginning to form in his head. Queen Cleopatra travelling beside him was worshipped as a goddess by many of her people. Caesar was now the most powerful man in the Western world. Caesar believed that he and Cleopatra could rule a huge empire, stretching from northern Europe to the Middle East.

Travelling in style

Cleopatra's royal barge was very luxurious. It was made from expensive cedar wood and cypress wood brought from the Middle East. The decks of the barge were covered with wooden arches. There was a special area for Cleopatra and her guests to sit. Inside, the rooms were furnished with beds and cushions covered in beautiful **silks**.

Shattered dreams

Julius Caesar stayed in Egypt for nearly a year. His **generals**, though, were becoming very worried that he was neglecting his duties in the Roman **territories** in the East. At the beginning of July 47 BC they finally managed to persuade him to leave Egypt – and Cleopatra. He travelled first to Asia Minor (now Turkey), and then back to Rome.

Caesarion is born

By this time Cleopatra had given birth to a baby boy, Caesar's son. She named him Ptolemy Caesar, but the people of Egypt gave him the nickname Caesarion, or Little Caesar. Soon after Caesar returned to Rome, Cleopatra sailed across the Mediterranean to join him. She took their baby son with her, and also her thirteen year-old brother and **co-ruler** Ptolemy XIV. She travelled with hundreds of servants and mountains of luggage. She was obviously preparing to stay in Rome for a long time.

▼ This carving at the Egyptian temple in Dendera shows images of Cleopatra and her first son, Caesarion.

Cleopatra in Rome

For the next two years, Cleopatra and her family lived in Caesar's huge **villa** on the banks of the River Tiber in Rome. She held magnificent parties where she entertained famous poets, musicians, **politicians** and other important people. Many Roman politicians were becoming very nervous about Caesar's ambitions. When he finally demanded that he should be made king of Rome, they decided that they had to put an end to him. On 15 March 44 BC, as he entered the **Senate** building, he was surrounded by a group of politicians who stabbed him to death.

▲ This is what remains today of the **forum** in Rome. The main Roman Senate building was here, and other buildings such as libraries.

Making friends

One important reason for Cleopatra's visit to Rome was to try to get the Roman government to make a new **treaty** of friendship with Egypt. This would help to protect her position. With Caesar's support the Roman Senate passed this new treaty quickly and easily.

Cleopatra returns to Egypt

When Cleopatra heard the news of Julius Caesar's murder she feared for her own life. She was so close to Caesar that she could easily have been the next person to be killed. As soon as possible she and her followers, including her young son Caesarion and her brother Ptolemy XIV, left Rome for Alexandria.

Octavian returns

Another reason why Cleopatra left Rome so quickly was that Caesar's **great-nephew**, who was also his adopted son, arrived there. His name was Octavian. He had been completing his studies in the town of Apollonia (now in Albania), but as soon as he heard of Caesar's death he hurried back to Rome. He saw the young Caesarion as a threat to his own plans to take over Julius Caesar's position as ruler of the **Roman Empire**.

▶ Because Octavian had been close to Caesar, he believed that he was the one who should rule the Roman Empire.

Back in Egypt

Soon after Cleopatra returned to Egypt, the young Ptolemy XIV also died. In Alexandria stories began to go round that Cleopatra herself must have had the young king murdered. Cleopatra wanted her own son Caesarion to be made king with her to increase her power in Egypt. It is highly likely that she really did have Ptolemy XIV murdered in order to get him out of the way. Caesarion was now crowned king, even though he was only three years old.

In Rome at this time the most important person was a brilliant **general**, Mark Antony. Cleopatra's enemy Octavian, however, was waiting for an opportunity to remove Antony from the picture. Octavian believed that only he should take Caesar's place as Rome's leader.

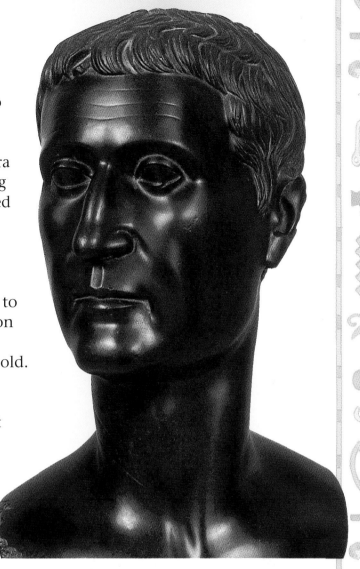

▲ After Julius Caesar's death, there was a struggle to decide who should be the new leader of Rome. Mark Antony, shown here, later shared power with Octavian and Marcus Lepidus.

Discontent in Egypt

Every year, the River Nile flooded. This was important, because it meant that enough food could be grown. For two years running, though, the river did not flood. The Egyptian people faced food shortages and starvation. Most Egyptians believed that Cleopatra was a goddess with powers over the River Nile. They blamed her for this problem. She became more and more unpopular.

21

Antony and Cleopatra

Power in Rome was now shared between three people: Mark Antony, Octavian and another **politician** called Marcus Lepidus. These three were known as the Triumvirate, and they divided control of the **Roman Empire** between themselves. Octavian looked after the Roman **provinces** in the west. Antony looked after the provinces in the east, and Lepidus took control of the Roman **territories** in Africa.

Antony sends for Cleopatra

Antony left Rome to take command of his territories in the east. On his way, he stopped at the city of Tarsus (now in Turkey). From there he sent a message to Alexandria ordering Cleopatra to meet him. He needed the support of Egypt to keep control of Rome's eastern territories. He also wanted to become Rome's only ruler. He hoped Cleopatra would give him money to help him. This was the chance Cleopatra had been waiting for. She wanted to return to the powerful position in the Roman world she had to give up when Julius Caesar was murdered.

◀ Cleopatra was a proud queen, as can be seen in this 1st-century BC marble statue. She knew how to use her power. When Mark Antony needed her help, she would only help him on her terms.

Cleopatra was not going to be ordered around by a Roman **general**, however. She was a queen who should be respected. Antony sent more messages ordering her to meet him in Tarsus. She ignored every one. At last she decided that she would go to meet him. She sent a message to say that she was on her way.

Antony meets Cleopatra

Some days later, Antony and his guards were in the main city square waiting for her arrival. A large crowd of people were also waiting to catch a glimpse of the famous queen. They suddenly began drifting away and moving towards the waterfront, while Antony and his guards were left alone in the middle of the square. Cleopatra had arrived and everyone had gone to watch. She came in a fantastic golden barge with purple sails. She was dressed up as Aphrodite, the Greek goddess of love and beauty, and she was waited on by her ladies. The year was 41 BC and Cleopatra was now aged about 29.

▶ Like Julius Caesar, Antony fell madly in love with Cleopatra. They lived together for several years, and had three children. This 17th-century tapestry imagines them together.

The brilliant actress

Antony was amazed when he saw the beautiful Queen Cleopatra arrive in her magnificent finery. He invited her to dinner in his palace but she turned him down. She said that, because she was a queen, he should visit her in her palace in Tarsus, which he did.

A new family

Mark Antony must have been dazzled by the sight of the queen in her boat. Like Julius Caesar before him, Cleopatra had captured his heart and he immediately fell in love with her.

Antony followed Cleopatra back to Alexandria and fell under the spell of Egypt. He returned to Rome in 40 BC, when he married Octavian's sister Octavia. In 37 BC, though, he sailed back to Cleopatra. Even though he was married to Octavia, for seven years he lived with Cleopatra in Egypt. They went on journeys up the River Nile and along the coast of the Mediterranean Sea, stopping in many beautiful palaces. They went on fishing and hunting trips.

Cleopatra's children

Cleopatra and Antony had three children. The first were twins, a boy named Alexander Helios (after the Greek god of the sun) and a girl named Cleopatra Selene (after the Greek goddess of the moon). The third was a boy named Ptolemy Philadelphus. They were brought up with Cleopatra's first son, Caesarion.

◀ Cleopatra and Antony's first children were twins. The boy was named Alexander Helios after the Greek god of the sun.

▲ This silver dish shows Cleopatra Selene. She was Alexander Helios's twin sister, named after the Greek goddess of the moon.

In the year 34 BC a magnificent **ceremony** was held at which Antony gave Cleopatra large parts of the eastern **territories** of the Roman **Empire**. Most of these lands had once belonged to Egypt, but they had been captured by the Romans. Since she first became queen, Cleopatra had wanted to restore the Egyptian empire. Now she saw her dreams begin to come to life.

Anger in Rome

Antony's behaviour shocked the people of Rome. He was acting like a king, giving away part of the Roman Empire to a foreign queen. Octavian now saw his chance to destroy Antony. He had already removed Marcus Lepidus from power. Now he spread stories that Antony had been bewitched by Cleopatra. The Romans knew that it was only a matter of time before Antony and Octavian would fight each other.

The death of Cleopatra

For the next six years, Antony and Octavian watched each other carefully. They both knew that there was no room for two leaders of the **Roman Empire**. Sooner or later they would have to go to war to decide who would win.

In 32 BC Octavian declared war on Cleopatra. He could not attack Antony directly, because Antony was an important Roman, but he could make war against Cleopatra, the queen of a foreign country. He knew that Antony would protect Cleopatra. Antony raised a huge army, and sailed with an enormous fleet and thousands of soldiers to Actium on the west coast of Greece.

The Battle of Actium

Octavian's navy trapped Antony's ships in the **harbour** at Actium for many months. Finally, on 2 September 31 BC, Antony's ships were able to sail out of the harbour to fight Octavian's navy. Soon after the battle began, though, 60 ships commanded by Cleopatra suddenly headed back towards Egypt. When Antony saw what was happening he sailed after Cleopatra. Abandoned by their commander, Antony's sailors and soldiers quickly surrendered to Octavian.

▶ This is the **prow** of a ship which was found on the sea bed near Actium. It may have belonged to one of Antony's or Octavian's ships.

Octavian chased Antony and Cleopatra to Alexandria. Surrounded and with few supporters left, Antony heard that his beloved Cleopatra had killed herself. He had now lost everything and so, in the noble Roman way, he fell on his sword and stabbed himself. But the news was wrong – Cleopatra was still alive. The dying Antony was brought to the queen, and he died in her arms.

Cleopatra was captured by Octavian's soldiers. Rather than become a prisoner she killed herself, too. Some people say she was bitten by a poisonous snake smuggled to her by a faithful servant. Others believe that she drank poison.

▲ This carving shows a Roman ship with its soldiers. Notice the **prow** at the front of the ship.

Why did they run away?

Why did Cleopatra order her ships to leave the Battle of Actium? Maybe she thought the battle was lost, and wanted to return to Alexandria to strengthen her army. Octavian later claimed that Cleopatra was a traitor to her own people, and said that Antony was a coward.

After Cleopatra

Cleopatra was about 39 years old when she died. Her dreams of a great Egyptian **empire** died with her. Soon afterwards Egypt was captured by Octavian's army and became part of the Roman Empire. As she had requested, Cleopatra was buried in the same **tomb** as Antony.

The last queen of Egypt

Her country may have disappeared, but the name of Cleopatra has lived on down the centuries. It still makes people think of romance, bravery and beauty. Cleopatra was the only **Ptolemaic** ruler who is respected as much as Alexander the Great himself. At a time when there were few women rulers, and when women usually had little influence, Cleopatra used all her skills to try to make sure that Egypt remained an **independent nation**. By doing this she made even the leaders of the powerful **Roman Empire** frightened of her.

◀ For all her rights and wrongs, no one can deny that Queen Cleopatra was one of the greatest ever rulers of Egypt. This statue is Roman.

► Much of ancient Alexandria now lies under the sea. Little by little, archaeologists are finding lost objects.

Before she died, Cleopatra had sent Caesarion away to safety in India, but Octavian's spies tracked him down. The young man was murdered when he was only seventeen years old. Cleopatra's other three children were taken back to Rome where they were paraded in Octavian's victory celebrations. They were brought up as Romans. Cleopatra Selene later married the King of Mauretania. We do not know what happened to the other two.

The lost tomb of Cleopatra

Over the centuries the tomb of Cleopatra was lost and forgotten. Conquerors came and went. The beautiful city of Alexandria was pulled down and built over. Parts of it now lie beneath the modern city. Parts have been covered by the sea. Recently, underwater **archaeologists** have begun to recover many statues and carved stones from buildings Cleopatra would have known. Maybe one day they may even discover the tomb of Cleopatra, the last queen of Egypt.

Glossary

archaeologist person who builds up a picture of the past by examining the remains of pottery, bones, buildings, writing and other records

ceremony formal event with special parts to it

co-ruler someone who rules with another person

dynasty family of rulers, in which power is inherited from one generation by the next

empire large group of lands ruled over by a single person or government

forum open space in Roman towns used by the public

general leader in an army

great-nephew son of a person's nephew or niece

harbour place where ships and boats can come in close to the land

historian person who studies and writes about things that have happened in the past

independent free from control

nation group of people organized into a single country that has its own rulers

philosopher someone involved with philosophy, the study of the world, the purpose of the universe and the nature of human life

politician person involved in government matters

province area within an empire, for example outside Rome but under Roman control

prow pointed part at the front of a ship

Ptolemaic rulers who belonged to the Ptolemy family in Egypt

Roman Empire the large area of Europe, the Middle East and North Africa controlled from the city of Rome between about 27 BC and AD 476

scheming someone who secretly plots to gain power and influence

Senate group of officials that governed Rome

silks expensive cloth woven from the fibres of the silkworm

successor person who takes over from someone else, especially a ruler

territory district or section of land

tomb building where people could be buried

trade buying and selling of goods, such as food

treaty formal agreement made between two or more countries

tutor teacher hired for a child at home

university place where many subjects are taught at an advanced level

villa magnificent house

will a legal document in which a person says how their property and money should be divided up after their death

Roman numerals (numbers)

The Romans did not have separate signs for writing numbers. They used letters instead. Here are Roman numbers 1 to 20:

I, II, III, IV, V, VI, VII, VIII, IX, X, XI, XII, XIII, XIV, XV, XVI, XVII, XVIII, XIX, XX

We use Roman numbers after the names of kings and queens to show how many people of that name have reigned.

Timeline

332 BC	Egypt conquered by Alexander the Great. He makes Alexandria the capital city.
305 BC	Ptolemy I first of the Ptolemaic rulers in Egypt
80 BC	Ptolemy XII, father of Cleopatra, becomes King of Egypt
About 70 BC	Birth of Cleopatra
58–55 BC	Ptolemy XII exiled to Rome
51 BC	Cleopatra becomes Queen of Egypt
48 BC	Julius Caesar arrives in Egypt
47 BC	Cleopatra gives birth to Caesarion
About 46 BC	Cleopatra joins Caesar in Rome
44 BC	Death of Julius Caesar
41 BC	Cleopatra meets Mark Antony in Tarsus
40 BC	Antony returns to Rome. Cleopatra gives birth to twins Alexander Helios and Cleopatra Selene.
37 BC	Antony returns to Egypt
31 BC	Battle of Actium
30 BC	Death of Cleopatra and Mark Antony. Egypt becomes part of the Roman Empire.
27 BC	Octavian becomes first Roman emperor with the name of Augustus

Further reading & websites

Heinemann Explore History – Ancient Egypt, Jane Shuter, Heinemann Library, 2001

People Who Made History: In Ancient Egypt, Jane Shuter, Hodder Wayland, 2000

The World of the Pharaoh, Anne Millard, Hodder Wayland, 1998

What Do We Know About the Egyptians? Joanna Defrates, Hodder Wayland, 1998

Heinemann Explore – an online resource from Heinemann.

For Key Stage 2 history go to *www.heinemannexplore.com*

www.egyptology.com/reader

www.thehistorychannel.co.uk

Places to visit

The British Museum, London

Index

Titles in the Life and World of series include:

Hardback   0 431 14765 5

Hardback   0 431 14771 X

Hardback   0 431 14774 4

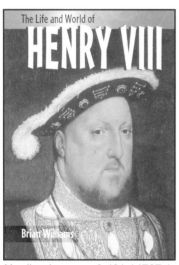

Hardback   0 431 14767 1

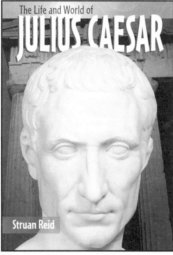

Hardback   0 431 14775 2

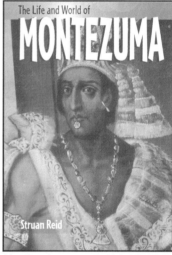

Hardback   0 431 14763 9

Hardback   0 431 14769 8

Hardback   0 431 14761 2

Find out about the other titles in this series on our website www.heinemann.co.uk/library